WITHDRAWN

St. Louis Community
College

These Were the Last

233/400 Townsend Godsey

U. S. Library of Congress Catalog No.: 77-88943

Godsey, Helen and Townsend

Ozarks Hill Folk

Published by

The Ozarks Mountaineer
Star Rt. 3
Branson, Missouri 65616

Printed in the United States of America
by Western Printing Co., Republic, Missouri

Typsetting by
ABC Publishing Services
1320-A N. Stewart, Springfield, Missouri 65802

Dedicated

to those old Ozarkers who kept

a sharp hoe and a merry fire.

INTRODUCTION

to the Ozarks and to the last of its native people.

A native Ozarker--one of These Last--was heard to say once, years ago, "There's two things a feller never hears in the Ozarks: the truth an' meat a-fryin'."

Until the middle of the Twentieth Century there was much substance to the latter of that hillman's disclaimers. It was a matter of economics. The first observation referred to an attitude of mind, which is still extant.

It is difficult to present either verbally or geographically a picture of the Ozarks and its vanishing indigenous people since the Ozarks is more a concept than a geographic reality. The Ozarks is "good or bad as thinking makes it so."

If you happen to look with disfavor on the region, you will feel inclined toward this story: It is said that after God became tired of building mountains and plains, He took the left over rocks and dumped them in one spot. And that's the Ozarks. (A discouraged early explorer who must have happened into the area in drab leafless winter or mid-summer's drouthy days, called them the "Desperation Mountains.")

Those of us more favorably inclined toward life in the hills as were the ancestors of the people in this book, prefer a different story. It seems a city dweller died one spring and went to heaven. He was appalled at seeing there a wild-eyed man chained to a rock. The newcomer, protesting to St. Peter about the doleful creature, was told that the man was from the Ozarks and that it was spring down there. "The only way to keep an Ozarker in heaven when redbud and dogwood bloom and the redhorse suckers are shoaling," said the good saint, "is to put him in chains."

Such an Ozarker would have found kindred souls among the persons photographed for this book, a people representative of the largest part of the population of the Ozarks of southwest Missouri and northwest Arkansas, at least until World War II.

SETTLERS CAME IN THE EARLY 1800's

The first settlers who came into the hills in the early 1800's were seeking cheap land and the freedom of new territory. They found 50,000 square miles of beautiful, almost uninhabited country now lying in parts of five states, though principally in southern Missouri and northern Arkansas.

This vast hilly tree and grass covered high plateau is laced with meandering streams which have serrated it over the centuries to produce ever deeper and deeper "gulfs" or valleys. The longest of the streams is White River which has many beautiful and historically colorful spring-fed tributaries.

The area comprises some of the oldest exposed land in North America. The better known Rocky Mountain uplift is believed to have pushed itself up 200 million years ago; geologists say that the Ozarks range is more than 500 million years old.

This domain of the Ozarkers, most of whom came from the Appalachian regions of Kentucky and Tennessee, is bounded on the north by the Missouri River and on the south by the scenic escarpments of the Boston Mountains in northern Arkansas. The region's easternmost edge extends slightly beyond the Mississippi River and its western edge is the Neosho River in Oklahoma.

White men, largely of Old American stock, were latecomers to the hills. Archeological finds indicate that prehistoric man lived in the Ozarks more than 10,000 years ago, the time of the mastodons, bones of which have been uncovered in several digs in the area. Clovis spear points made by the paleo-Indians of the same era, also have been found.

Bluff dwellers were in the Ozarks more than 1500 years ago and findings of pottery, clay pipes, fragments of baskets and fabric confirm the presence of the late woodland Indians from A.D. 500 to 900. No one seems to know what happened to these people.

Earliest written records of Indians of the Ozarks plateau began with explorers' accounts of the Osage Indians. The Osage lands were acquired by the U. S. Government after the Louisiana purchase, and the Indians were moved into new Indian Territory farther west. Cherokee were ceded land in northern Arkansas in the early 1800's but they too, were moved on. Delaware and Shawnee Indians as well as several other migrant tribes lived in the area for brief periods.

In 1838, the year of the removal of Indians from their eastern homelands, many Cherokee traveled through the Ozarks on what they called "the trail where the people cried." A few straggling Cherokee dropped off along the routes and there are descendants of these proud people still living in the region.

GREAT BEAUTY FOUND IN OZARKS MOUNTAINS

French and American explorers, trappers and traders came into the area before the arrival of permanent settlers. In their journals they extolled the region for its great beauty and natural wealth. They wrote of woods lush with wild fruits: plum, persimmon, pawpaw, red haw, service berry (shadbush); strawberry, huckleberry, dewberry, and blackberry. Trees with edible nuts: chinquipin, walnut, butternut, beech and hickory were reported. A wealth of beautiful and useful trees were listed: dogwood, redbud and deciduous holly, pine, black and white oak, yellowwood, cottonwood, sycamore, gum, ash and cedar.

A very special tree, the Osage orange, abundant in the Ozarks at that time, is thought by many researchers to have given the area its name. Early French Canadian trappers found the Osage Indians making excellent bows from its wood and called the region "Bois d'Arc" meaning bow wood or the land of the wood for bows. This French phrase was gradually corrupted to the word Ozarks.

Another version of the naming of the region is that it was a corruption of the French phrase Aux Arc, which referred to the many bends or bows of the streams meandering through the hills.

The Ozarks hills embrace the highest land between the Appalachians and the Rockies although they are not as high as is often assumed. And to settlers of a century and a half ago, these hills were as deceiving as they are today to the more than sixteen million tourists coming here in all seasons for sightseeing, camping and water recreation, folk and crafts festivals. (The current popularity of folk lore and the proliferation of successful old time music and crafts festivals attest the interest in and the validity of recording in environmental portraiture these survivors of a self-sufficient people.)

This broad irregular dome which is the Ozarks has its eastern apex among the granite boulders southwest of St. Louis, Missouri. Taum Sauk mountain in St. Francois County, 1772 feet elevation, is the highest point in the state. However the average elevation in the Ozarks is 800 to 1000 feet though some hills rise to as much as 1400 feet in southwest Missouri and 2,500 feet in northwest Arkansas.

Here and there knobs or "balds", a surprising sight, rise out of the landscape. Balds are high rounded treeless hills often covered with tall grasses or low shrubs.

While possessing not quite the height of the Appalachians from which so many of the early settlers came, nor the grandeur of the Rockies which few had ever seen, the Ozarks of the White River and its tributaries have about them a picturesqueness and restfulness that is satisfying and enduring. Anyone traveling through the mountain regions of Tennessee, North Carolina and Kentucky, if he were familiar with the Ozarks, would surely understand the feelings of the pioneers as they ventured into this area, that they were coming into a new homeland. The eastern mountains are slightly higher than the Ozarks but there is an atmosphere, a feeling, that is unique to both regions.

Even the modest heights of the Ozarks furnish breathtaking views. Perhaps this accounts for the fact that most of the early roads and highways developed along the ridges.

Once an imaginative westerner was riding along one of the ridge roads with its lovely vistas. As the road descended into the hollow below to the usual small settlement, the traveler mused aloud, "You know, these Ozarks hills are different from our Rocky Mountains in more than just their lesser height and lush greeness. Out there you go uphill and come down; but here it is more like you go downhill and come up." It is when going downhill or entering a deep hollow or gap that the illusion of mountain height is encountered.

The Ozarks hills may not satisfy the definition of mountains, that they rise at least 1000 feet above the surrounding terrain, but their height was significant enough to adventurers and pioneers afoot, to be mighty wearying. And they created barriers that closed off the settlers from the outside world. Ozarkers lived in virtual isolation for nearly a century in what geographers and sociologists term an arrested frontier.

Yet if one may judge from the lives of These Last, who were early Twentieth Century descendants of those Ozarkers, they must have been a people contented with their lot. They were imbued with the spirit of freedom; they were resourceful and fiercely independent. The general westward movement bypassed them, but whatever the development of surrounding areas the Ozarkers' pride and independence intensified through the years.

SPRINGS AND CAVES ABOUND IN REGION

The region is rich in springs with some 10,000 recorded in the Missouri Ozarks alone. Major springs number more than a hundred, 98 of them having a flow of more than a million gallons of water a day. Big Spring in Carter County (on Current River) is the largest single spring in America. Its flow has been measured at as much as 840 million gallons in a day.

The most spectacular springs in the western Ozarks are Roaring River, in Roaring River State Park, which flows 28 million gallons a day; and Bennett Spring, also in a state park, about 100 miles north of Roaring River. It normally flows an average of 96 million gallons a day. Blue, Blanchard and Mammoth Springs are notable in Arkansas.

Many of the springs throughout the Ozarks were sites of early waterpowered grist and saw mills. There are more than 250 mill sites recorded in the Missouri Ozarks alone and as late as the 1920's there were 125 waterpowered grist mills in operation. Today there are less than a dozen in the entire area.

The Ozarks embrace at least 1,400 surveyed caves some of which have yielded bones of ice age animals. Most are inhabited by some species of bats. Several of the larger caves have been known to Ozarkers for more than a century and a number of them were used as shelters for both man and beast. Early settlers excavated guano, the excrement of bats, from some of the caves, using it for fertilizer or boiling it down to produce saltpeter. They mixed the saltpeter with pulverized charcoal and sulphur to make gunpowder.

Alluvial lead was so common in some areas of the hills that pioneers could pick it up off the ground. Using resinous pine knots which burned very hot for the smelting fire, they melted the metal in hollow stumps and used it to make rifle balls. A number of small lead mines were operated for a time along streams large enough to provide transportation. In the western part of the Ozarks lead and zinc have been mined by at least three generations of Ozarkers.

The earliest white men who came into the Ozarks came by river--up the White. They were adventurers, explorers, or hunters and trappers involved in the fur trade. If they stayed in one place at all, they lived as squatters and few made any contribution toward the settling of the area. By 1840 immigrants were beginning to come overland.

LARGE GAME ANIMALS ONCE WERE PLENTIFUL

Wildlife of the Ozarks was originally abundant and of great variety. Excessive trapping for the fur trade had taken a heavy toll by 1840 but wild game remained the main source of meat for the settlers for nearly a century.

Henry Schoolcraft, who came into the Ozarks on a mining exploration in 1818-19, wrote of life among those few earliest people who had ventured into the territory: ''The food at the hunter's camp of Holt and Fisher consisted of hominy, bear bacon, sassafras tea and ditany or spice tea. The hunters brought into camp the leg bones of some buffalo for the marrow, cracked the bones with an axe and took out the marrow.'' He also reported that by the time a boy had reached the age of fourteen he had learned the use of a rifle, the arts of trapping beaver and otter, how to kill bear, deer and buffalo and to dress out the skins for making footwear and leather clothing.

The once abundant buffalo, antelope and elk were gone by the mid-1830's but bear, deer and wild turkey remained abundant. Bear were killed and butchered for hams, for fat (often rendered for oil) and for hides. Deer were hunted for their meat and hides. Small game such as racoon, beaver, fox, wild turkey, dove, quail, wild duck and geese also furnished much meat.

It was within the memory of many of the hillfolk shown in this book that both large and small game were plentiful throughout the Ozarks.

Pioneers were pleased to find on the meadows of the high plateaus and knobs, grass so lush that wild animals could hide in it. Even livestock was sometimes difficult to find in the tall grass but it was valuable forage.

River cane grew in profusion in the lowlands and provided winter shelter and forage for livestock and big game such as deer and bear.

Most of the pioneers, especially those from the Appalachians who were agriculturally minded, chose to settle in the narrow valleys of the upper White River basin. Rich, narrow strips of valley land most of which is now covered by lakes, was the first to be claimed by the settlers.

Along a stream was the logical site for settlers' cabins, and settlements and trading centers quickly developed in the valleys or ''gulfs'' as they were called. Limited but productive farming was possible in these valleys.

Life was not always pleasant for the Ozarker any more than it ever is for anyone. In addition to the normal ups and down of life, hard toil and doing with so little (in many cases living at subsistence level) there were adjustments to make to strange surroundings and a capricious climate.

The Ozarks is subject to occasional periods of severe heat, cold, drouth and floods. Normal seasonal temperatures range from 21 to 100 degrees. Rainfall averages 40 inches, one half of which comes in the summer months. It often occurs as severe thunderstorms with torrential ''gully washers,'' creating high humidity and severe erosion of overcut hillsides.

The prevailing wind is westerly or southwesterly. Average killing springtime frosts occur about April 15 along the Missouri/Arkansas border. October 17 marks the average first frost in the fall. This provides a long growing season of 200 or more days, if moisture is adequate.

PIONEERS FIND PLEASANT CLIMATE

Such a climate made reasonably manageable living for the pioneers. The secret of good life in the hills, they soon learned, was the ability to adjust to their environment. Those who adjusted their lives to nature instead of trying to force nature into their accustomed ways, found life pleasant, if rugged.

Life was particularly good in the spring, early and late summer and in the fall. Mid-summer was too hot and dry for maximum enjoyment and winter days could be very dreary.

Spring has always been the loveliest season in the Ozarks. Long before the balmy days of April, strange green things begin to push up out of the earth. Later an abundance of flowering trees and shrubs burst forth: service berry, redbud and dogwood, spicewood and pawpaw. Early spring flowers, bloodroot, adder's tongue, trillium, spring beauty, hepatica, buttercups and violets, wild verbena, phlox and firepink, to name a few, carpet the earth with a riot of color. The hills abound in such a variety of plants that the Ozarks is a treasure trove for the botanist, herbalist and the granny woman.

Early Ozarks women, too long held at the hearth by wintry weather, joyously abandoned the confinement of their cabins when soft breezes and swelling buds betokened spring, and sallied forth to gather some of those strange green things for "sallet." Redhorse shoaled and folks caught enough for rollicking community fish fries. This was the time for a round of sassafras tea to thin the blood and a mess of poke greens to awaken winter-dulled appetites; a time to dig up the garden patch for planting and tap maple and hickory trees for sap which was boiled down for a sweet syrup.

Everyone liked an Ozarks spring.

In early May when the wild blackberry canes burst forth into white bloom, looking like drifts of snow, there comes a spell of chill weather usually followed by warm, balmy days. Now and then the brisk season is severe enough to dash hopes for an abundant wild fruit harvest. The hillfolk named this time blackberry winter.

Summer was the season when early gardens finished off and corn, wheat, cotton and tobacco, which were the main crops, grew and matured. (In the 1900's the people pictured herein grew grapes, strawberries, tomatoes and beans as cash crops.) A "fall" garden was planted in late July or early August.

Summer brought hot days but the nights were usually cool. If there was an occasional unbearable night, beds were moved into the yard under the trees. And fortunate indeed was the man whose cabin was in a cove near a cave entrance where a "down draft" was nature's own air conditioner.

Fall rivals spring as an ideal time in the Ozarks. Many think September and October, when brilliantly hued leaves flame against deep blue skies, the finest months. Nature daubs reds, yellows, bronze and purples over the abundant oak and ash trees; over maples, sycamores, hickories, black and sweet gums, that tower over fiery sassafras and sumac. Patches of deep green cedar, by contrast, heighten the bright colors.

As the days shorten into winter, the landscape begins to brown. Winter usually is not unduly severe but contrasted with other seasons it is bleak. An Ozarks winter has an average of only 11 days when there is a measurable amount of snow.

As fall and winter merged, pioneers began to prepare for chill days to come. They repaired the chinking of cabin logs and daubed fresh clay between fireplace rocks. They cut and stacked firewood.

Provident settlers butchered meat for smoking--venison and bear hams as

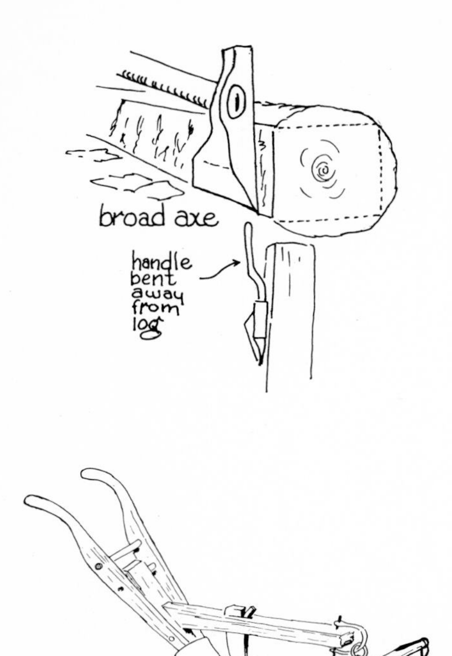

well as pork, if they had it. If they made sausage it was put down in lard in large gourds or encased in corn shucks and smoked. They robbed bee trees for honey and beeswax, taking bees for their own bee gums. A man with a crop of cane, cut, stripped the leaves and squeezed out the juice and boiled it down into sorghum which they called "long sweetenin'."

Most fruits such as wild strawberries, blackberries, gooseberries, service berries, wild plums and cherries had to be used in their season but apples, peaches or pears, when available, could be sun dried for later use.

Late garden produce was harvested and stored. Pumpkin and squash were sliced into rings and dried on strings suspended from kitchen beams. Onions, their tops plaited, were hung on cabin walls and root vegetables were left in the ground or put into straw pits or crude stone cellars.

Despite the fact that the women of These Last had canning jars they could use, most of them followed many of the customs of their ancestors in drying and storing vegetables and fruit. It was less trouble, the product more tasty to them and took up less storage space.

Wealthy and contented was the man whose woodpile was high, who had products of the growing season stored on shelves or under the bed, whose smokehouse held plenty of meat and whose young hens were beginning to lay. There were those who so managed during other seasons that in winter they could do as the brown woodchuck and hole up for the lean months. If they ventured out from the warmth of their hearth it would be to tend livestock, run a trapline or join in a neighborhood fox chase or 'coon hunt.

PIONEER'S NEEDS SIMPLE AND FEW

Chief needs of pioneers and settlers other than products of the field, forest and stream were salt, gunpowder, calico bed ticking, and a linament that served both man and beast. As the region developed, these necessities could be obtained by barter of herbs, furs, wild honey, beeswax, bear grease and tobacco at trading posts or settlements which stocked what a homesteader might need.

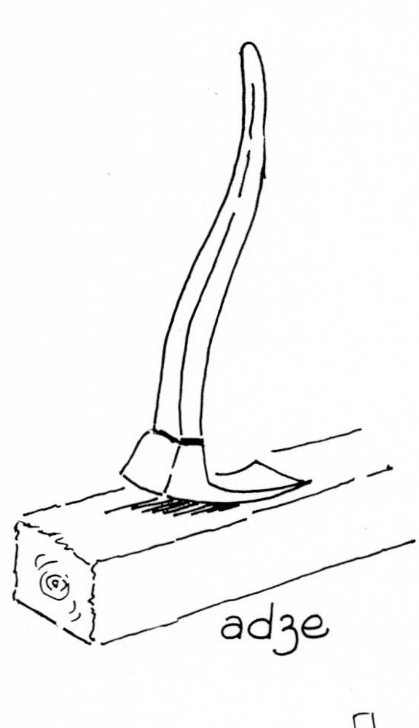

A pioneer brought with him to his new home an axe, a grubbing hoe and a bull tongue plough or a turning plow. These were important for clearing a site and preparing the land for planting. For cabin building he needed to bring an iron froe for making shakes, a broadaxe for squaring logs, an auger and a saw. He might later acquire an adz and chisel for better shaping and dressing wood and a few other desirable tools as he could afford to buy them or for which he could barter his labor. For harvesting he needed a reap hook, scythe and cradle. He could make a flail for winnowing and a three-tined wooden pitchfork for stacking straw and hay.

Many of the folk shown in this book were born in log cabins which their ancestors built--dwellings made of scalped logs or logs hewn square with a broadaxe and fitted at the corners with chamfer and notch. Spaces between the logs were chinked with clay. Moss, lichens, straw and even hog or other animal hair were used for binding. Peeled poles served as rafters and the roofs of the buildings were shingled with shakes. Cabin building techniques used by the Ozarker even in the late 1800's were identical to those used in Virginia, North Carolina and New England during Revolutionary War days!

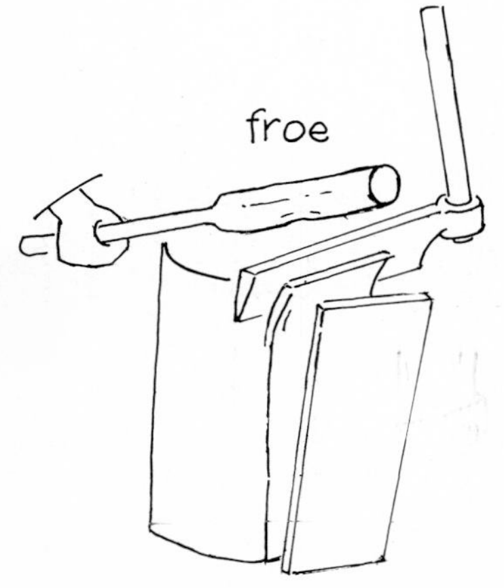

Shingles or shakes as the Ozarkers called them, were made with the froe, a blade about a foot long and three and a half inches wide with a round hole at one end where a handle was inserted. This blade was set upright near the edge of an upended bolt (a 24 inch section of tree trunk) of oak or cedar, and struck with a mallet to split the wood lengthwise into shingles about one half inch thick and five or six inches wide.

Shingles must be split during the dark of the moon lest they curl up at the edges, causing the roof to leak. To prevent splitting they were put in place, when fresh cut, with a single homemade nail. They were laid on the rafters snugly, side by side, and the first rain swelled and tightened them.

Cabin doors were made of split (rived) timber adzed or dressed down with a drawknife and secured with leather or wooden hinges. The latch was inside the door and could be raised from the outside by means of a rawhide thong put through a hole above the latch. The latch string was drawn in at night. (Here is the origin of the current expression of hospitality that "the latch string is always out.")

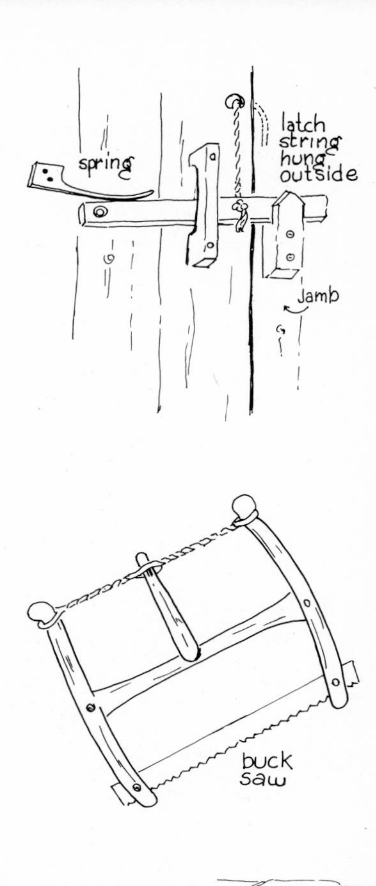

Early cabins were rectangular units about 10 to 15 feet wide and 16 to 20 feet long, called pens. Their size was limited by the length of logs available and how heavy a timber could be handled. If more space was needed as the family increased, an additional unit was built nearby. The roof and sometimes the floor were then extended to join the two pens making a "dog trot" between them. In some instances a lean-to kitchen of rived boards provided additional room.

Floors were of tamped earth or split logs pounded into the earth, cut side up, to make a puncheon floor. The rounded sides of the logs were mauled into the earth or laid on sleeper logs. The flat, split sides of the logs were smoothed with an adz.

Pioneers constructed their fireplaces of small green logs plastered with a red clay mixture or they used flat sandstones put together with mud mortar. Later fireplace chimneys were built of field stone held in place with fired limestone mortar.

On cold nights when a heavy fire was needed a member of the family must stay up to keep watch over the fire for the mud chinking dried and fell out exposing the wood which caught fire. In such an emergency an ever ready bucket of water was doused on the chimney walls.

Cabin furniture included a corner bed with trundlebed, and perhaps a free standing cradle. Or a cradle-box was sometimes attached to the wall above the foot of the bed. The bed was little more than a bunk built into a corner of the cabin, the fourth corner being attached to a post. Mattresses placed on homemade rope springs were stuffed with corn shucks, straw or feathers.

Small children often slept in the corner bed with their parents or in the trundle bed. Older children slept in the loft on a pallet laid down on boards across the rafters up under the roof. Holes were made in the cabin wall and fitted with pegs driven in at right angles to serve as a ladder to the loft.

Children, both boys and girls, wore long dresses and were called "shirttail youngens" until they were about five years old. To keep a child from underfoot in so small a living space a mother would "bedpost" him. This meant putting the child's dress tail under the free corner post giving him reaching freedom but not roaming room.

Additional furniture in a cabin might include an all-purpose table and a highbacked ash or hickory chair or two. Three-legged stools for stability on an uneven floor were common. Utensils included a cedar churn, a cedar tub, and a "piggin" as a water or milk pail was called.

A Kentucky rifle (actually a muzzle-loading rifle made in Pennsylvania) or a musket, commonly hung over the fireplace or above the cabin door. Other important items were an iron pot and a skillet with short legs, called a spider, a corn gritter and a greased board. This latter was called a johnny-board for on it johnny cakes (a coarse cornbread) were baked before the open fire. Very few Ozarks cabins had cooking-pot cranes, cooking being done largely in the short legged pot or spider set in the hot ashes or coals. In warm weather cooking was done over an outdoor fire.

Skins were used for rugs and for bed covers. There were few windows in early cabins but when a hole for one was cut, it was covered with a skin scraped very thin.

Dishes were scarce in most early cabins. Gourds and wooden trenchers were adequate substitutes; sometimes there were spoons made of horn or wood. A few families had molds for making lead or pewter spoons. Tin cups were available but were definitely a luxury item.

buck saw

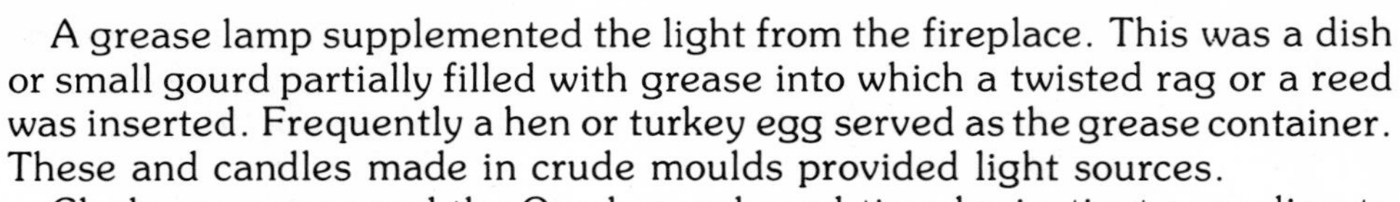

A grease lamp supplemented the light from the fireplace. This was a dish or small gourd partially filled with grease into which a twisted rag or a reed was inserted. Frequently a hen or turkey egg served as the grease container. These and candles made in crude moulds provided light sources.

Clocks were rare and the Ozarker reckoned time by instinct according to when sunlight shining through the doorway fell across a certain plank on the floor. A day was reckoned as from "kinsee to cain't see."

The cabin home of a more affluent pioneer or homesteader might have a set of carding combs and a spinning wheel for making yarn and a loom on which the women of the household could weave homespun cloth for the family. The cloth, called linsey-woolsey, was colored with homemade natural dyes. Most of it was much of the same color, usually brown, dyed mainly with walnut or butternut hulls. As time became a little more relaxed the women experimented with various plants, roots and bark and developed green, mustard, yellow and purple dyes. Woof for the loom thus dyed was used to weave colorful stripes into the material. A garment of linsey-woolsey was scratchy but it was very warm.

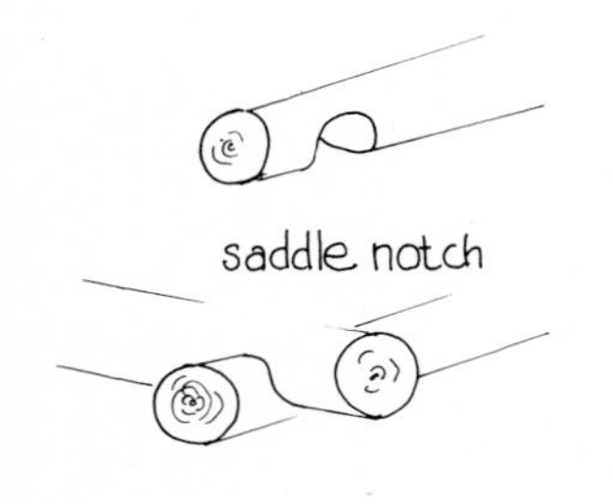

As the pioneer developed his homestead a smokehouse was one of the first outbuildings to be added. (until he could build a smokehouse the earliest settler often fixed a meat box to store salted meat inside the cabin.) A typical smokehouse was a windowless 10 by 14 foot long log room with a narrow door. Here meat was hung to cure in the smoke of a slow burning hickory fire built on the earthen floor.

The floor became very hard from the fires. In bad times, dirt from the floor was sometimes dug up and boiled to recover the precious salt that had dripped from the curing meat.

Following the curing season the smokehouse was used also as a storehouse for sauerkraut, seed corn, beans, apples and other foodstuffs including lard, wild honey and sorghum kept in large gourds. If there was a good spring flowing nearby, a small wooden or stone building called the springhouse was built for keeping perishables, especially in summer.

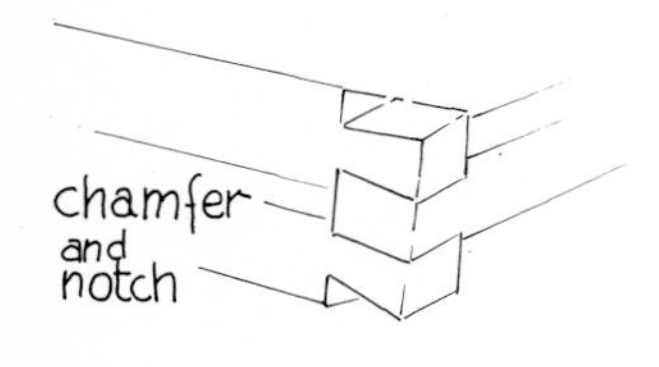

Enjoying the untrammeled freedom of the vast open spaces of the hill country with its abundance of wild fruits, fish and game, the Ozarker harvested many bounties of the land. His garden, however, required protection from marauding animals and this created a need for fencing. A rock or brush fence as a by product of land clearing was the first sort. Then a paling fence of poles or pickets was used around the pioneer woman's kitchen garden. Finally the Ozarker built a rail fence "horse high, hog tight and bull strong" to keep in his own livestock and keep out range animals. Barbed wire fencing was little used in the hill country until well into the Twentieth Century and many an Ozarker, in his laissez faire attitude, branded hogs and cattle and let them range the woods to forage for food.

There were no limiting game and fish laws in the wilderness but extravagant killing of wildlife was not common. An animal was killed chiefly for meat, grease or hides. Yet having no stringently enforced state or federal laws did not make this a lawless area. "Chimbley corner" or common-consent law, provided a definite code of conduct. Any breech of the code was severely punished often by the person against whom an offense was committed or by a committee of "regulators."

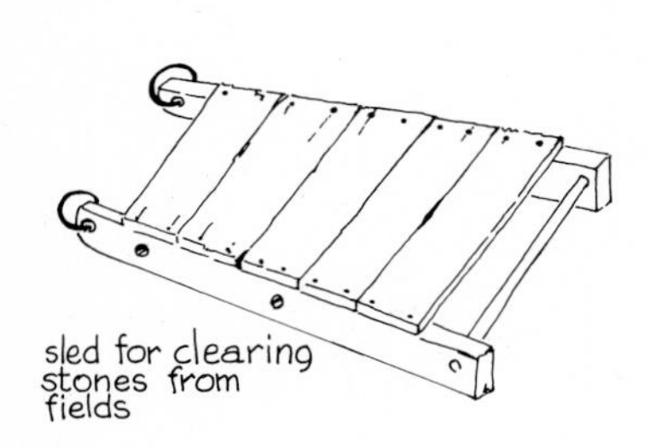

Somewhere beside each free-flowing stream there was usually a watermill where corn was ground on buhrs imported from France. These grinding stones were used as ships ballast on an ocean voyage, unloaded at New Orleans and transported up river to a convenient point. They were then hauled overland to the mill site in two-wheeled ox-drawn carts. Milling, one of the world's oldest industries, was the Ozarks' first. Liquor distilling was the Ozarks' second industry and it was a natural development from the availability of ground corn used to make mash.

Later, at watermill sites, cotton was ginned and baled for shipment to market. Other early industries were tanneries and blacksmith shops, both important to their communities. Some blacksmiths were very versatile and skilled men, capable of doing a variety of metal work and woodcraft. They built cradles and coffins, did gunsmithing, gravestone cutting and even bone setting and tooth pulling!

For the agriculturally minded homesteader trees were barriers to progress, a nuisance, something to be destroyed in the hard work of clearing land for cultivation. Larger trees were used for building cabins or animal shelters or were split for fence rails and firewood. But tree cutting eventually came to be a source of income.

Cedar was cut and shipped for making pencils and fenceposts. Walnut was snaked out of the woods by oxen and used to make lumber for fine furniture and for gunstocks. Hickory was sold for furniture and barrels, pine for building construction, oak for flooring and bridge timbers and railroad ties. Hundreds of thousands of ties for rail lines all over the United States were hacked annually during the late 1800's and early 1900's by hardworking hillmen who received from ten to forty cents a tie for their labors. Until the early 1940's few families could claim an annual cash income of as much as $300. Barter was a common means of local commerce.

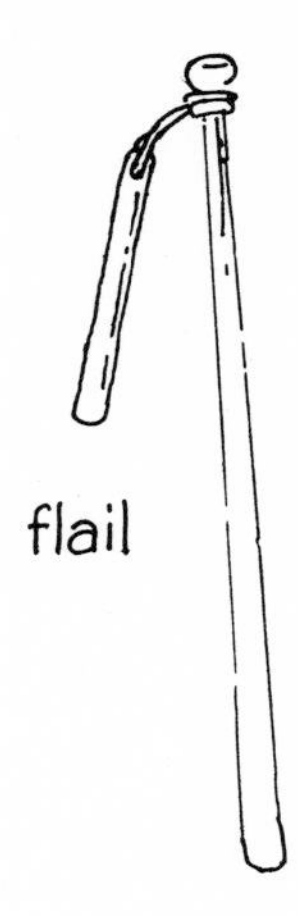

RELIGION-EDUCATION SOCIAL LIFE BEGINS

In their original isolation hillfolk's work, religious training and schooling were all home centered. As the number of settlers coming into the region increased and they could claim "neighbors," however distant, socialization naturally developed. Shared work in land clearing, cabin or barn raising became social events. Soon there were quilting bees, corn shuckin's and bean hullin's.

Meeting together in homes for religious worship or, in likely weather, under a brush arbor, became another means of socializing. The brush arbor was a shelter made by trimming four small trees as corner posts of a large rectangle about twenty by thirty feet. Four slender trees were cut and trimmed and put from post to post making an outside frame and across these were laid a roof of leafy boughs to provide protection from the sun and rain. Worshippers sat on split logs or rough board benches. It is thought by some that the Ozarkers' brush arbor may have had its origin in the custom of booths of Old Testament times, or perhaps its use was learned from the Indians.

Brush arbor meetings were usually held in August or September after the early crops had been harvested and fall gardens beginning to grow but not yet ready for harvest. Souls were "saved" during the enthusiastic preaching, hymn singing, testifying and praying, the latter often in tongues. Foot washings and baptisings in a creek were usual follow-up ceremonies of brush arbor meetings.

Hillfolk put great emphasis on informal religious worship and avoided involvement in an "organized" church. Fifth Sunday meetings and basket dinners were joyous events.

Religious leaders were usually unschooled men who had "seen the light" or were "called" to preach. They were men with a gift of oratory and a great love for and familiarity with the Bible.

As communities developed, an occasional circuit rider visited the area. His coming was an event of special significance. An old witticism of the hillman was that "if you hear something coming through the cane it's sure to be a bear or a preacher."

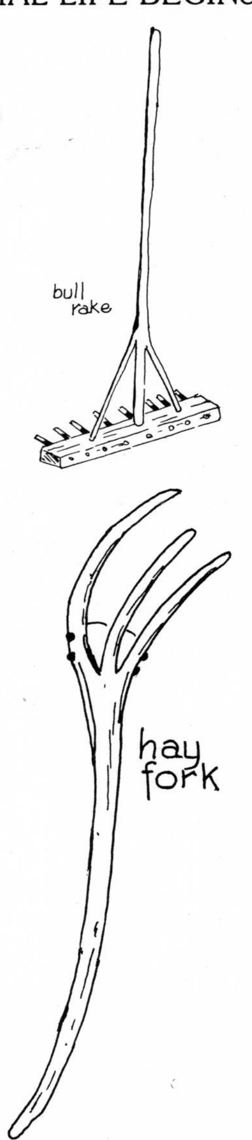

The first schools were subscription schools and provided the only education available to hill children until the late 1800's. To have a "scripted" school, each family with children of school age had to pledge a given amount to pay the teacher. The first teacher was apt to be a parent or a local young adult. He or she was chosen if thought to be bright, of some education and marked ability to maintain discipline and a will to work for a meager salary, often as little as $15 to $25 a month. The teacher, when not a local resident, was usually a man who was boarded around and was expected to be of some help with chores to pay for board and keep. Sometimes he was also a preacher.

A subscription school teacher was often contracted for only a month at a time and a school might have several teachers during a single term. Terms were short, usually no more than three or four months in length. Moreover, a term might begin at any time during the year and end whenever the children were needed at home to help with planting or harvesting chores, or when there was no money to pay the teacher.

Classes were conducted in a one-room, two-window school built of logs or rough sawed boards. Slanting shelves along the walls served as desks for the pupils who sat on rough puncheon benches. A bench set in the front of the room was the recitation bench. On a slightly raised platform was a simple rough-lumber table used as teacher's desk and the painted blackboard was hung or nailed to the front wall. A fireplace or a potbellied stove furnished heat if it was needed. The water bucket was wooden and had a gourd dipper out of which everyone drank. This building also served as the church meeting place and as a voting place.

Until 1912 pupils were classified according to their reading skills and were promoted by readers rather than by grades. A pupil might be in the sixth reader without having mastered comparable skills in geography, arithmetic or any other subject. In the one-room school, however, due to the constant reinforcement from hearing others recite, many children learned verbal skills quickly and well.

SOCIAL LIFE CENTERS AROUND SCHOOLHOUSE

The social life of an Ozarks community soon centered around the schoolhouse. Spelling bees, cyphering matches, writing and singing schools were all a part of the education incentive and were also fine opportunities for socializing. In the late 1800's following the establishment of county district schools, debates, elocution contests and pie suppers were popular forms of community entertainment.

Further socialization developed with the advent of play parties and square dances. They were held in a host's cabin on a Friday or Saturday night.

On these occasions music was furnished by a fiddler and perhaps a banjo or guitar player. Frequently someone beat out the rhythm on a jawbone. Because the fiddle was the common instrument for dancing parties which often became very rowdy, it was considered an instrument of the devil and was long banned from use in churches throughout the Ozarks.

There was little free day time for Ozarks children since they were included as early in life as possible in all work necessary to family survival. Such playtime as there was, was employed in strictly no-cost activities and developed mainly as products of their imaginations.

Boys entertained themselves with tree climbing, fence walking, exploring the woods, bragging, or playing follow the leader in a dare-devil braggadocio fashion. They went swimming and fish noodling or played mumblety-peg and sometimes marbles, games that even menfolk often played.

Mumblety-peg was a knife-flipping game of considerable skill and marble playing developed at times into a serious skill-challenging game. Nearly every small town and some county seat towns of the late 1800's and early 1900's had a marbles playing ground. Whittling was a popular pastime for men and boys, too. For the men it was almost a social pastime, something to do with their hands as they sat talking with each other.

Girls, in their playtime, played house, counting games, hull gull (a guessing game) or jumped rope to the sing-song rhythm of old rhymes and counting chants. Timeless delight was the hours spent playing with dolls however crude they might be (though a few surviving examples attest to considerable ingenuity and creativity on the part of a loving grandmother or favorite aunt). Dolls were whittled or made of natural materials such as corn cobs or corn shucks using cornsilk for hair. An especially coveted one was the beloved rag doll made from a precious scrap of calico and likely stuffed with home grown cotton from the quilt garden.

PLAYTIME

During holiday seasons, men held shooting matches for prizes of beef or turkey. Shooting for beef was straight target shooting but a turkey shoot was more involved. The turkey was hobbled behind a log and contestants stationed some distance away. The order of shooting was determined by drawing lots. As the turkey flopped around, now and then sticking its head above the log in response to a call being used by one of the men, it made a sporty target. Firing continued in rotation until the bird was finally killed; the luckiest or most skilled marksman carried away the turkey as his prize.

There are a few records of an occasional gander pull among the younger men but as the community grew less rowdy the sport was frowned upon. A gander pull involved staking out in an open field a goose whose neck feathers had been liberally greased. A rider with his horse at full gallop leaned down and attempted to yank off the goose's head. The rider who beheaded the goose received it as his prize.

Young hillmen and women began dating early and most were married by their eighteenth birthday, many much younger. A wedding was invariably followed by a charivari (shivaree) or serenade. This event publicized the marriage state of the couple and also was an occasion for gifts of food to help stock the newlyweds' larder. Frequently the shivareers hazed the couple by dunking them in a pond or nearby stream.

GRANNY WOMEN, LIFE AND DEATH

Protesting babies were ushered into the world of the pioneer by granny women whose art had its roots in the practices of the "wise women" of old England. Granny women served as physicians to the isolated hill people. They had a store of mysterious simple remedies and superstitions handed down from generation to generation of pioneers. A few of these remedies were traceable to the Indian's use of medicinal herbs. Most of These Last had been delivered by granny women.

Hillfolk buried their own dead and most communities had a woman skilled in laying out a corpse. She closed the eyes of the dead, placing coins on the lids to hold them shut; she tied a cloth under the chin and over the top of the head to hold the mouth closed. These were left in place until rigor mortis set in. She bathed the face with wahoo bark tea and camphor to prevent discoloration of the flesh. Washing and clothing the bodies of women and children was her task but a man was expected to bathe older males.

Many an Ozarker kept boards in his hayloft against the day neighbors would be called in to make a coffin for him or a member of his family. By the late 1800's coffin materials such as sateen for lining and cotton lace for trimming were staples in many stores. These items were still available in isolated areas as late as the 1940's. In the earliest settlement years a simple winding sheet or even a quilt had sufficed. Many of These Last participated in traditional hill burials and some were buried in homemade coffins.

The "bury hole" was dug by friends and relatives of the deceased and a grave was never left open overnight lest it claim another member of the family. As soon as possible after a death lest their bees die, too, or go away, a family member went from beehive to beehive telling the insects of the death.

The clock was stopped, the mirrors, if they had any, were covered, cats put under a basket or tub and the pillow of the deceased carefully opened in hopes of finding an angel crown.

Funerals were held as soon as possible after death. (Facilities for embalming a corpse were not available to most hill folk until well into the 1900's.) A funeral might last two hours or longer and often two preachers took turns sermonizing. At the graveside service, friends stood up and testified to the virtues of the deceased and neighbors took turns with the shovel, to fill in the grave.

In general, older hill folk held to these and many other traditional ways well into the Twentieth Century.

In the preface of one of his many books on Ozarks folkways, Vance Randolph said of the Ozarkers that they were "the most deliberately unprogressive white people in the United States. Descendants of pioneers of the Southern Appalachians, their ways of life changed very little during the whole span of the Nineteenth Century. They lived in a lost world where primitive customs and usages persisted right down into the age of industrial civilization."

OZARKERS RESIST BEING "BEHOLDEN"

It went against the grain of these typical Ozarkers to be beholden. Even in rationing days of World War II they resisted "signing up" for butter, meat and sugar stamp books. Long sweetening and wild honey were used to avoid signing for sugar. Meat for the table was as varied as ingenuity and hunting skill could provide. An old Civil War period substitute for coffee--parched grain or parched cubed sweet potatoes--was often used, and scarce food for which the Ozarker couldn't find an inexpensive substitute, he did without.

These fiercely independent people once had a feeling for superior English; their speech was lyrical and they had a great store of picturesque sayings and superstitions.

Settlers before 1860 were predominantly of Scotch-Irish extraction and by way of the Appalachians they brought with them numerous Scotch and English ballads. Such a one was:

> Willie, sweet Willie
> Oh, Willie farewell:
> I'm going to leave you
> I love you so well.

Until they were exploited by cartoonists and entertainers, hillfolk did not object to being called "hillbillies" and often used the term themselves. They brought the term with them from the Appalachians where it appears to have originated as a further endearment of the term hillwillies, an affectionate expression women of the mountain country of Kentucky and Tennessee used for their men.

Hillbillies had a great sense of humor, usually humor of character which often was pungent. Humor of character is personal and to be effective requires that the hearers know the victim of the joke.

Hillbillies took delight in "gulling." Gulling was in effect play-acting of the most realistic sort. If a stranger was within hearing, two or more hillmen would strike up a conversation with each other in deliberately audible tones. With great exaggeration they would rehearse or vividly tell an oft-reported happening. Their demeanor would be so serious and they seemingly so oblivious of an audience, the gullible stranger would be completely taken in. Such duping was wry fun for the natives and it gave them a sense of superiority over the gulled outlander.

Their everyday humor was droll humor, sly and sometimes off color, more closely related to British humor of understatement than to the traditional American frontier humor of over statement. Nevertheless they were capable of telling tall tales.

Hillbillies might have seemed funny-turned at times but they were not the buffoons or comic strip characters often pictured by cartoonists, Hollywood movie producers or country music entertainers.

Hillmen had a strong sense of family. They staunchly defended the virtue of wife, daughter and hound dog though not necessarily in that order. A good boy was one who was good to his mother.

As outlanders began to come into the Ozarks to live, settlers became clannish. They fought among themselves, over the most trivial of matters such as the spelling of a family name; but they resented intrusion by another and invariably united against outsiders, sometimes violently turning upon an innocent bystander. These hillfolk asked only to be left alone and allowed to "stomp their own snakes."

Native Ozarkers were suspicious of "furriners" and not without cause, for some outlanders who came into the area on business took advantage of them. First it was fur, beeswax and yarb (herb) buyers; then land speculators, peddlers and bushwhackers. There were timber buyers and railroad tie buyers and later, range hog and cattle buyers. Egg, fruit, cotton and tobacco buyers came. As they had little, if any, means of transporting their produce to a favorable market, hillmen were at the mercy of unscrupulous traders.

It was natural then that Ozarkers became suspicious of all strangers. In later years there was the added fear that the stranger might be a game warden looking for poachers or a federal agent hunting moonshiners or one to tell them how to run their farms.

Hillmen transferred their deep suspicions of outsiders whom they felt threatened their freedoms, to new settlers and it took a long time for newcomers to prove themselves and be accepted. Even today, though Ozarkers are overtly courteous and respectful, an outlander is seldom fully accepted into whatever remains of the Ozarkers' fragmented society.

Considering their experience with outlanders, it is not surprising that hillbillies became as sharp bargainers as the proverbial New England Yankees. It is said of one family that on a rainy afternoon their menfolk could go out in the barn lot and make five dollars each just trading knives among themselves. In business dealings, however, These Last were honest folk whose word was bond. Once they had "shook" on a deal it was considered final and inviolable. No written word or signature was needed.

EXTERNAL FORCES CHANGE OLD WAYS

Rugged old Ozarkers, having learned to live in relative harmony with nature and to wrestle a simple living from the hills and hollers, survived the Nineteenth Century. They had endured the vagaries of the elements year after year. They had survived the ravages of the Civil War and the maraudings of bushwhackers. They had coped with the entrepreneurs who would exploit them and their labor.

As they entered the Twentieth Century these hillfolk strove, against increasing odds, to maintain their stubborn independence.

With the coming of the railroads and highways early in the 1900's, however, strong pressures from the outside began to change their environment. Forces beyond their control were encroaching, slowly but irrevocably, upon their isolation.

Ozarkers loved their country and were quick to defend it but they had no love for any "gover'ment feller." For them the government was always suspect. Yet when the great depression of the 1930's brought nation wide social programs to the hills, Ozarkers found themselves at the sufferance of the federal government. It was frustrating and eroding to their independence.

The call to military service and industrial war effort in the 1940's took many hill people, especially younger ones, out of the region. When they returned to the hills they found more outsiders coming into their territory. They were beset by forces completely beyond their control, forces which drastically changed the state of their world.

Thousands of acres of the better lands in the valleys of the Upper White River Basin were being inundated behind flood control and hydro-electric power dams. As the lakes rose the Ozarks became a vacation land, a playground. Soon young folk were abandoning hard scrabble agricultural efforts to go to work in better paying tourism related jobs and services.

An ever greater number of vacationers and retirees, augmented by urbanites seeking refuge from mounting problems of the cities, came pouring into the area seeking water recreation or the simple way of life which many believed the hillfolk were still enjoying. Ozarkers ultimately found themselves a minority in their own country.

If you come to the hills today, you will not see many of such people as are shown in this gallery of photographs because THESE WERE THE LAST.

MODERN ERA BRING FOLKLIFE CHANGES

The culture of a region is never a static thing. It is ever-changing--even in so long isolated a region as was this domain of the Old Ozarker. Change is accelerated by external forces and in just two generations the folklife of the Ozarks hills has been transformed to the worryfull, complex mode of modern living.

The hills continue to provide a haven for those who wish to leave time be; to those who appreciate the restful and satisfying beauty of the region. Life is still folklife and the Ozarks continue to undergo acculturation which is contributed to by each new wave of immigrants, largely retirees, tourism related entrepreneurs and representatives of government agencies.

The inevitability of change diminishes the need to try to preserve (except as a fact of history) the pioneer way of life as represented in the lives of These Last. It is more important that the lands and waters which the old Ozarkers held dear but of which, in their unknowingness, they were such poor stewards, are made environmentally secure for generations to come; that redbud and dogwood always can bloom against clear blue skies and that St. Peter still will find it necessary to use chains to keep departed Ozarkers in heaven, come greenup time.

--Helen and Townsend Godsey
Branson, Missouri - 1977

UNCLE WYLSE YANDELL became a weather-turned man from more than half a century of running a ferry on White River.

Wylse and his wife Sally lived in a log house within "hollerin' distance of the ferry." When Sally complained about Wylse spending so much time with curious visitors, he replied, "Folks come down here in the Ozarks to see a hillbilly and I ain't one to disappoint 'em."

The ferryman

Always friendly but never taken in even by radio or movie personalities who sought to exploit him, Uncle Wylse knew who he was and maintained his dignity.

Until the mid-1900's Moore's ferry provided one of the few means of vehicle crossing White River from Missouri to Arkansas.

AUNT CASSIE WHEELER

AUNT CASSIE WHEELER--butter maker

Adella Casandra Wheeler lived out her 87 years in the log cabin in which she was born. She had the reputation of being the maker of the finest sweet cream butter in the country. She used a cedar churn with a long handled dasher for years until the REA came and her children bought her an electric churn. She continued to use a hand whittled butter spade and a crock, however, to work the last vestige of water from the butter. She sold her butter in the nearby village.

The Ozarker's resourcefulness grew out of his isolation and the necessity in his formative years of his looking out for himself.

"I'd like to see the city some day but I don't reckon
I'd like to live where there's no woods or creeks."

"Hits hard to plow a straight row in a hilly country and a feller and his team gets bone tired."

Family ties were strong and hillfolks married for life.

There was nothing like the cooling waters of a spring fed stream on a July afternoon.

"An' that's how the Ozarks was when I was a little small boy."

"Tomater pickin's a lot of hot work."

TOMMIE REDFEARN--expert Ozarks sorghum maker.

In a make-do society survival depended upon a pioneer's ability to use resources at hand rather than upon ''store boughten'' goods and foodstuffs. The hillman's persistence in growing his own cane and making his own sweetening (called sorghum in the Ozarks and always referred to as ''them'') made it possible for him to have an energy making sweet for his cornbread, biscuits or gingerbread, or, mixed with butter, his ''striped butter.''

Once nearly every community in the hills had at least one sorghum maker as typified by Tommie Redfearn and his wife Peggie. They were among the last of the old time sorghum makers and their kind is not likely to be seen again.

The sorghum makers

Son Homer brought in the fresh cut cane from the hillside field.

The cane, stripped of its leaves, was pressed of its juice in a primitive iron roller mill powered by a horse pulled sweep.

"Long sweetenin's got to taste just right," always cautioned Peggie Redfearn before she allowed the cooking to stop.

The thin green cane juice was slowly reduced to rich golden molasses when cooked in long pans over a steady wood fire. Natives called the squeezed out cane stalks in the foreground "pummies."

Once the sorghum was cooked right to the taste it was poured out into lard cans to cool. (The Redfearn's forefathers used large hollowed out gourds to store molasses.) Later they were transferred to syrup pails for sale.

The Redfearns also made long sweetenin' for their neighbors keeping a part of the sorghum as their "toll."

Sometimes those who left the hills remembered to write.

MARY ELIZABETH MAHNKEY was a sensitive writer of lyric poetry. Her country correspondence won her a trip to New York City where Mayor Laguardia gave her a ship-in-a-bottle. She treasured that gift the rest of her life.

"I've picked many a stick of type for our little weekly," explained MRS. DUNLAP who carried on after her husband had put to bed his final edition of the Winslow Mountain Echo.

Maple or hickory sugaring provided a source of sweetening as long as the maples and hickories survived the lumberman's axe.

"It takes a passel of bi'lin' to make a stirrer of syrup."

A sharp blade on the cradle, a certain rhythm, strong arms and a long day were necessary for harvesting grain.

UNCLE JIMMIE WHEELER was still as rugged as an Ozarks oak when he was well into his 80's.

Hilda, the last log postoffice.

“Mail’s got light these days.”

Do-si-do--and around we go! "A fiddle and a good hound shore pleasures a man."

The hound dog men

In a hillman's scale of values three things have been held inviolate--his wife, his daughter and his hound, tho not necessarily in that order. An old judge once said that more blood has been spilled in the Ozarks over dogs than for any other reason.

An Ozarks fox chase was a social event with the hunters, man and boy alike, gathered around a cracklin' fire on a high moonlit knob after having turned their hounds loose. They spent the night listening to the high pitched voices of their hounds in pursuit of old reynard over the wooded hills and up the coves. It was all for the sport of the chase. The Ozarks fox hunter was content with fellowshipping around the fire, perhaps warming his insides with a swig from a jug, thrilling at the chase, and forbidding the trapping or killing of the quarry.

Not so with the coon hound man who, while reveling in the chase, expected his hound to pay for its board and keep by treeing the 'coon. After the 'coon had been shaken from its retreat the dogs fought and killed the little bear so that its hide could be stretched and sold at a profit.

Some hillmen still keep a hound--fox or 'coon--most often out of sentiment. With the passing of open range and the coming of extensive cattle grazing, tree defoliation, barbed wire fences, subdivisions along the streams and lakes has also come the end of the old ways of the Ozarks hound dog man. The full cry of a hound on a hot scent is now a rare sound, a ghostly cry out of the past.

"I thought I heard my little bitch real close."

Judging of the hounds often preceded a race with such experts as Emmett "Ragfoot" Adams as the authority.

"Them hounds 's still a-runnin'."

"Come brother, set a spell and rest yore hat. I'd make old Bugle move out'n that cheer but he run all night and yore a-lookin' at a tarred hound."

"Ever man ought to have a good hound."

"Fox huntin' is running yore hounds all night and looking for 'em the next two days."

A good coonhound might bring as much cash money as a man could earn in a year.

The coon hunter measured the success of his sport largely by the number of hides on his cabin wall.

"A body can be plum nelly proud of a span of white mules."

THE BEE HUNTER: "There's nothin' like wild bee honey and alumn to cure a cold."

"Hits real sport to course a wild bee from a bait of honey and anise to a hive tree."

The bee hunt

The Ozark bee hunter's equipment was simple: a smoker, a bee hat, a pail of bait, a choppin' axe and a saw.

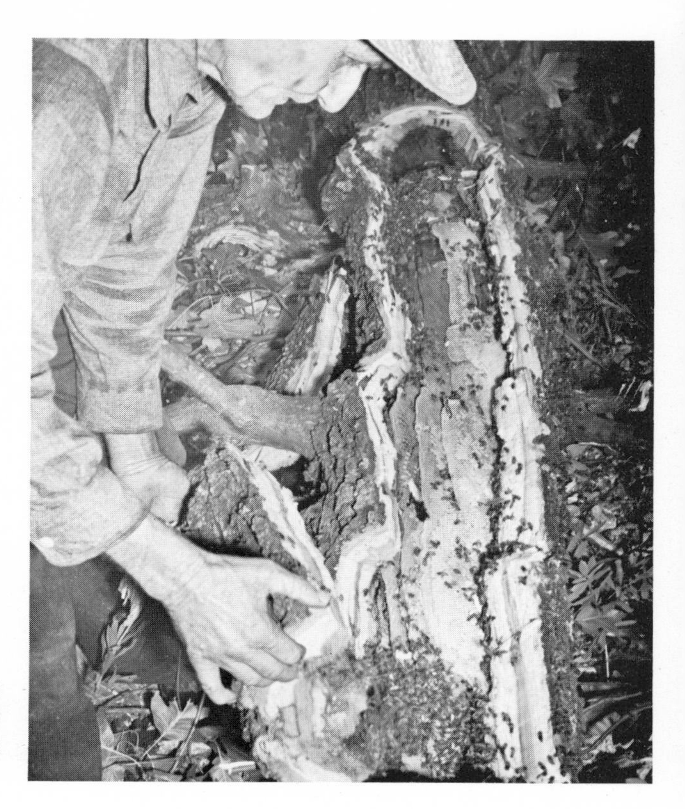

"In old times afore the big trees were felled and bees killed by poisons aimed at killin' insects, a feller might get a hundred pounds of honey from a single tree."

"There's nothin' tastes quite so good as warm honey and comb from a bee tree."

"The youngens all like wild bee honey almost as well as long sweetenin' or brown sugar."

"Women folks are proud to get bee honey for eatin' and cookin' and they put it up, comb and all, in fruit jars. Our grandma put it up in a holler gourd."

"In those days a body took a bait of corn to the water mill for grindin' on the stone buhrs."

With the passing of old ways also went the oxen, the last of their breed in the Ozarks. These patient animals were especially important to the homesteaders because one ox had the strength of twenty horses.

FAYTE BOYD--Master hickory splint basketmaker.

The basket maker

A good basket required good craftsmanship.

"My youngens learnt basket weaving by watching."

Splints were shaved from a piece of hickory held in a simple vise.

The craft of basket making survived even if the old masters didn't.

"OLD MATT'S" CABIN--The most photographed building in the Ozarks is this restored log cabin which is one of the last of its kind in the hill country. Here a preacher named Harold Bell Wright was inspired in 1906 to write the romantic novel, "The Shepherd of the Hills" in which he sought to portray the already vanishing breed of hillfolk.

Many Ozarkers brought their love for good horses from their old Kentucky homes.

J.M. NICHOLS, Mt. Judea chairmaker. True Ozarks crafts were crafts of necessity and chairmaking was no exception.

“I shore hated to see that old ivy covered stone church that served us for more than three quarters of a century have to be tore down stone by stone on account the flood waters of Bull Shoals lake.”

Strawberries were a great cash crop in the Ozarks until workers were lured into service jobs when the new lakes brought the resort motel boom.

"We earned our school supply money berry pickin'."

THE STATE OF THE NATION interested the Ozarker less than the condition of his crops. The native had a great love of his country but remained suspicious of government.

Tobacco was once a big crop in parts of the Ozarks but when allotments were set interest waned. Only a few Ozarkers such as LIJE JACOBS held on and he was the last.

Children never cared much for tobacco raising--the blossoms had to be topped and the tobacco worms killed.

Nearly all of the wells in the Ozarks were located by means of witching sticks. Few Ozarkers now claim the power to find good water sources by means of the divining branch.

Market day in a make-do society brought out unusual make-do vehicles.

FRANK SHAFFER, country correspondent

The country correspondent

FRANK SHAFFER--Chronicler of Protem

When pioneer residents of a White River village at the east edge of Taney County Missouri couldn't agree on a name for their post office the postal service labeled it PROTEM. The name lasted for more than 80 years. The old village is gone now to make way for the flood plain back of Bull Shoals Dam and the post office is located in a grocery store on higher ground.

Principal chronicler of the isolated village was Frank Shaffer a one time school teacher who wrote a weekly country correspondence column for the **Taney County Republican** for many years. A sensitive man, he had a lyric style of writing about happenings among his neighbors and their environment in the little community that had its name "for the time being."

Protem on a typical afternoon in May.

Frank's beat was his village.

exerpts from the Taney County Republican

Protem News

Ellen Coiner, Grandma Adams, and Lottie Blair heard a wild varment on the bluff last night and Ollie Smith heard it, too, but thought it was a hen a-choking. Others thought it was a wampus cat. Where is your dog, Jourd Jenkins?

Mrs. Beatrice Shaffer received her 100 baby chicks in good shape by mail. She will be found at home now. Thanks.

Uncle George Coiner's hands hurt him. Using the hammer too much each day and kept it up for 80 years, pity, pity. He is 92 years old and commenced shop work at 12 years.

They had services at the Brown School the 30th. Had a very large crowd and four preachers. Rev. George Shaffer, Rev. Hiram David, Rev. Frank Stuart and Rev. Sturgis were there and all had a big dinner.

The little wrens are so happy. Their gourd home is so snug and dry.

Uncle Zephy Dunn is no better.

Willie Holt was in town, was able to ride his horse and is a-mending a little. Said grass was good.

Smile! Smile! The greatest month of the year. The Ozark hills are so beautiful, the wild flowers, the little wrens, the great mocking birds songs, the sweet little busy quail with her attractive sweet obedient family, her weeping willows, her moaning pines, her cool bubbling springs, her rolling rivers, her blue stem grass, her hollow trees and big poke stalk greens, the big terrapins, with their good house with them. I have three but they have not come home yet--not taxed--Thanks.

Saws and axes are making music on White River for the big monster lake. Pity, pity, pity the big pawpaws are gone, the fat ground hogs are fleeing to the high hills. The monster is taking possession. Farewell.

O,O,O! Had distinguished visitors. Edgar and Rachel Lawson and son Glen of Highlandville. I stayed with the Lawsons when I taught school at Highlandville. Our good deeds live after us. We certainly enjoyed their company, too. Rachel brought one of those luscious cakes, mm,mm--and fried chicken, too, Thanks!

Oh, those good showers of rain.

He which soweth bountifully shall reap also bountifully. II Cor. 9:6.

Washday, brush burning on White River, house wood, canning and haying, fishing, busy, busy, busy. School is full.

To Grandma Adkinson (dead) I thank you too for helping in that great brush arbor revival at old Dirt Dob. Thanks.

Aunt Ellen Coiner took a dizzy spell while seeing about Uncle George Coiner and she fell and hurt herself and Mrs. Smith and others had to help her up. High blood pressure.

Aunt Julia Adams got cold and bought herself a big load of good wood.

O, say, I'm looking for my 3 little lost terrapins. Now they want neither a house nor a bed. They have them but they will be glad to have a big ripe cantaloupe for supper. Thanks.

Monday Morning. Standing by the big water oak stump sawed off about 4 feet high and 3 feet across the top, sawed off near the big springs about 1/4 miles from the old Adams house watching an old quail with a big bunch of baby quails. O she is a honey of a mother, she is very watchful and good to her little ones, and two pet heifer calves and a foster mother (heifer) with a big bell on are here for a drink out of the clear cool spring. (Oh what a sight.) And Mart McCall's big fine fat white faced bull is lying in the shade of a big water oak tree--come for a drink. The quails are well fed by the little red berries on the buck bushes and on the Indian Turnip berries. Yes, the two pet calves get a little lunch from the little heifer. She is grazing on the big rank rag weeds (O, their lunch is bitter). Please excuse us and we will do better next time.

Charley Sowards (Orb's brother) is very low. Mrs. Attie Ragsdale is improving right well.

Aunt Cindy, age 84, wears an attractive smile and has two big, red, ripe, tomatoes in each hand. Thanks.

Lo, I am with you always, even unto the end of the world. Matt. 28:20.

Mrs. Oda Aldridge is not so well.

Lottie Blair is a little better.

Grandma Adams is about the same.

Mrs. Clifford Brown is real sick but some better.

Elige Jennings are all sick.

Mrs. Anna James is no better.

Measles, Measles, Pity, Pity. Everybody has them. Nobody wants them.

To Aunt Sarah Adams (dead) Come unto me, all ye that labor and are heavy laden, and I will give you rest. Matt. 11:28.

You surely were tired when you reached my mother's bedside on that old horse following that dim dark path after giving birth to eleven sons and daughters and with child seven months (no doctors). Thank you Grandma for helping deliver me into this world, December 21, 1880.

O,O,O, Mother Eve, your light is still shining and I'm still wondering where your dear body is. I love you. I find you bore three sons, first, Cain; second, Abel and third, Seth. Then you are forgotten (wrong). Adam lived 930 years, died--Gen. 5:4. Where is Mother Eve. She didn't get justice. No, excuse me.

I can't find words sweet enough to say to you virtuous, loving never tiring darling, mothers and virgins. You are comfort; you are Angels. Our life saviors. You are a powerful body if you would stay together thirty years. Will you? I believe in justice. Mothers and Virgins, please take a deep thought.

Aunt Hester Rhodes (sleeping) I want to thank you a thousand times for being so good to me while I boarded with you and you only charged me $4.00 per month. Thanks.

O,O,O! such a beautiful day. I'm sitting in the little garden, the little birds are so happy. The little wren has her nest about eight feet from my chair. I cut a hole in a big gourd just about big enough for her to get in and cleaned it out about four inches from the bottom. The gourd is real crooked and can't get into the nest and I hung the gourd to a crooked limb on a peach tree with wire about six feet from the ground. It swings but nothing can bother her. She's gentle. She gets her feed in the gourd. Thanks.

Listen, listen, Up Jenkins' dark alley at that big wooly hoot owl in that big water oak tree. (hollow) Come back Wolf.

Protem is sure in hot water now, for the old dam is going to take us, and no place to go. We have to leave our old grave yard and our new church house. No place like home sweet home. Stay at home. Our boys are gone and our girls in grief. Pity, pity.

To Henry Jones (blind) and Aught Rozelle, the old river farms where you have worked so hard have already been under water by the big Bull Shoals dam and a rise in White River but the dam is filling now and out of the fields.

My wife, Pearl, has promised me a big Rhode Island young rooster and big eggs for dinner Sunday. I hope I can rise early mm-mm. Tie the white and black kitten up so I can get the liver. Thanks, honey Pearl.

Good luck and bad luck. Ed Drake's big black dog chased something from their hen house down the bluff and treed it. But Ed didn't take his gun. The dog treed either in a big leaning hollow tree or in the hole in the bluff and was standing on the tree about six or eight feet from the ground barking with all his might and snapping at something. Ed was laying at the lower end of the tree where it went into the dem in the bluff. Ed either had the buck ager or scared or lost his grip for a red fox jumped into his arms and Ed let it get away. It was after Aunt Cindy's hens or ducks.

To Aunt Jo Gray (dead) of Cedar Creek. How I love you for the many, many good things you did for me. On August 10, 1911 at 12 noon on the bank of White River you assisted Dr. Bowlinger of Lead Hill, Ark., and delivered a big bright eyed baby girl, weight 9 pounds, named Mattie May Shaffer. Thanks, thanks, very much. You were a good mother and grandmother and an excellent cook. I am proud I had so many big good ripe water melons under the bed for you both to eat. Thanks to you and George and Tom.

O,O,O, I went out into our little garden to get some big chunks of wood for my wife to wash and there under the chunk near our house was a big copperhead snake. I grabbed my sharp hoe and cut off his head and then I hit him again and cut another piece off of him. Ray Tinker, you and others know how bad I did swell when that copperhead bit me at Walnut Shade about 28 years ago, on the left hand and finger. I used coal oil, yes, lots of it.

Please use coal oil if a snake bites you. Thanks to all of you who assisted me in my awful pains.

I believe in reflex action. O, I sure hurt now, but I'm not bit.

--Frank Shaffer

"A feller's down on what he ain't up on."

Anyone running for county office soon learned that to carry the eastern township he must take his message to Tobe Nave's store.

"Sometimes a body likes to set a spell and just remember!"

Tobe Nave's store, filling station and post office was a principal center of communication and here Frank was able to pick up items of news and gossip for his column.

The post office was in the back of the store.

Frank often mentioned TOBE NAVE in his column because the storekeeper usually knew who in the community was ill, having a new baby, or had received mail order chicks, seeds or word from a relative in some distant place.

Getting mail was an event in Protem.

Even the village cemetery was on Frank's beat.

The Sycamore Log Community Church is one of the very few surviving log structures in the Ozarks. Most old log buildings, especially the squared log cabins of the 1800's, have been acquired and restored by area theme parks.

TOM YOCUM, last of the old White River float guides, spent a lifetime hunting for a Yocum Dollar, a fabled Ozark coin that supposedly "contained more silver than the government dollar." Tom liked to smoke a good cigar impaled on a matchstick which he held in his teeth in order to smoke it all.

In the true Ozark practice of giving expressive names to things and actions, the point for starting a float trip was called the put-in.

The float trip

Originating out of pioneer times, float trips on White River became popular with the evolution of the old river pirogue into the 22 foot long john boat capable of carrying two fishermen and their guide.

The meandering river, once teeming with game fish, the john boat and colorful native guides provided outlanders with recreation and allowed a lucrative business to develop over three decades. Then came the dams converting White River into a series of lakes where speed boats took over from the john boats and time took its toll of the old guides.

They're all gone now--river, boats and guides--and live only in the memories of those lucky few still alive who remember what is past never to return.

As head guide, Tom ran the commissary boat ahead of the float party.

Tom was a good camp cook and liked to work alone.

When outlanders discovered float fishing which long had been enjoyed by Ozarkers, the recreation thrived as a big business until dams converted the choice float streams into lakes.

“Hits shore a pleasure to whack off a windy for strangers. I think they like it.”

The late Robert Paige Lincoln, nationally known outdoor writer, interviewed Charley for a john boat story.

CHARLEY BARNES built more than 300 john boats for use on White River and its tributaries.

TED RICHMOND--depression days homesteader

Twilight Ted . . . homesteader

While homesteading 160 acres of some of the wildest land in the Ozarks Ted Richmond brought book culture to the backhills. But land speculators and promoters of mid-century made life so miserable for him because of his stand favoring conservation that he was forced to leave his beloved hills and his Wilderness Library.

Nevertheless, for a while he left his mark upon the minds of many hillfolks. The bookman, who sometimes wrote a column or verse under the name of ''Twilight Ted'' shared his small log cabin with his library and his goats. Seven rugged paths led to the library where hillfolk came to borrow a season's supply of good reading material.

A steady stream of books came in response to hundreds of letters from book reviewers and other booklovers throughout the United States. They supplied him with more than 25,000 books and many magazines for his library. Mrs. Franklin D. Roosevelt was one of his most famous contributors and after her husband's death sent a large number of the president's books to Ted who toted them two miles down the rocky Mount Sherman trail to the Wilderness Library.

Ted lived a simple life with his books and his goats.

Books for the Wilderness Library came via Mount Sherman post office two miles away.

Hillfolk walked miles to the Wilderness Library for a season's supply of reading material.

The last log schoolhouse was gone by the mid-1950's.

The last log schoolhouse

A footlog on the trail to the school offered possibilities for fun.

"Youngens learned to read an' spell an' cypher in our country school."

School sometimes lasted three months.

The pie supper

At an Ozarks pie supper "WhatamIbid" was the starting cry of the auctioneer as he held aloft a gaily decorated box containing a pie whose maker's identity was supposed to be a secret until the bidding was over. The highest bidder ate the pie with the girl who brought it.

A program, rehearsed for several days in the schoolroom, always was performed before the auction. It helped build suspense.

"A pie supper night is a frolicksome time and the kids get to show how good they've learnt to sing."

Pine Top school on the Missouri-Arkansas border was one of the last one-room country schools where pie suppers were held.

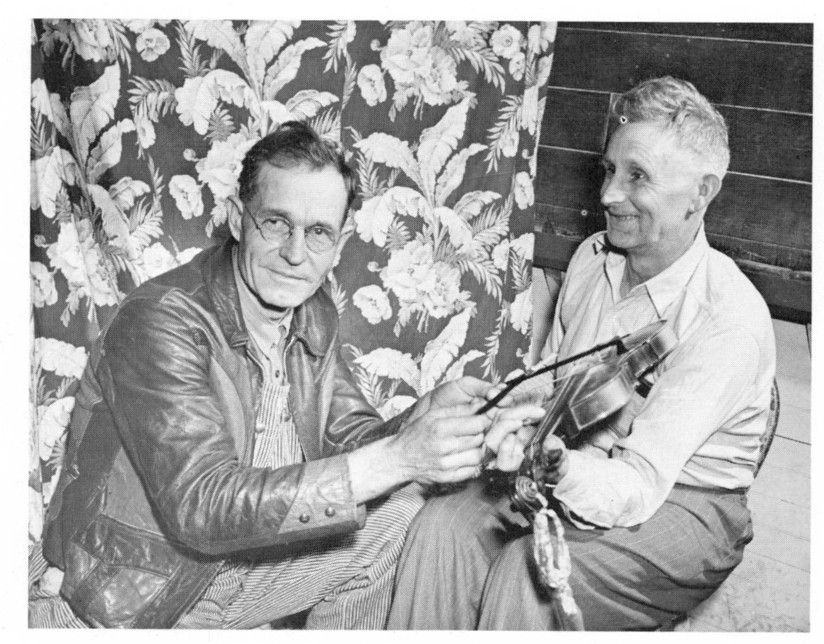

While the fiddler sawed with a bow, a partner used knitting needles to beat out the rhythm on the fiddle strings. "Not many fellers know how to do it anymore."

“Fun’s in gettin’ to eat the pie you bought with the girl who brought it.”

A square dance in a cabin--a kitchen sweat some folks called it--was a Saturday night social event.

The kitchen sweat

In the old days parents took their children nearly everywhere they went.

A cold kitchen stove might provide a seat for a guitar player.

With floor space limited to only one set at a time dancers took turns in the fun and frolic.

VANCE RANDOLPH, "Bull Goose" of the Ozarks folklife collectors, recorded hundreds of folk tunes and songs on heavy equipment loaned him by the U.S. Library of Congress. He has gathered thousands of items of folklore including folk speech, superstitions, and tales from which he produced scores of books during his more than half a century of traipsing the hills and hollers of the Ozarks.

"DEACON" HEMBREE liked to play the fiddle almost as much as he liked to tell tall tales to fishermen he guided on float trips. He always ended his stories with "Hit's the truth, porely explained."

FIDDLIN' JAKE VINING liked to saw off a tune for tourists.

MAY KENNEDY McCORD, a native ballad singer and chronicler of life in the hills, "The Lord willin' and the creek don't rise"

The shape note singers performed a cappella.

The folk festival

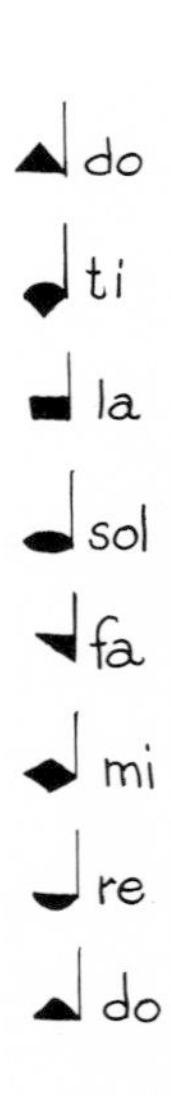

The St. Joe folk festival by and for Ozarkers was held in a bluff shelter.

Ozarkers didn't have a dance, they had play parties.

Some Ozarkers did fancy fiddlin'.

The last of the old Ozarkers still knew Elizabethean "ballats" from the auld country.

AUNT SUE MULLINAX--grannywoman: "Law, mister, I brought a passel of youngens into this world; reckon I couldn't norrate how many."

Where there was a horse there was a Hodges...the last of them being FRANK HODGES, past 90, who was able only to sit out his years in his "office" and remember the glory days of the Hodges' fox trotters and fox hounds which the family brought up from Arkansas.

“Yes, we’ve got a boy but he’s way out west in Joplin,” explained B.F. CRANFIELD of near Protem who, with his wife, lived out their years in the manner of pioneers. This highly resourceful man was preacher, “cheer” maker, blacksmith, crib and coffin maker.

He used an Arkansaw stone to keep his mowin' blade sharp.

Using a beeler maul made from a redbud trunk hardened by standing in the fireplace corner, Cranfield split ash bolts for making eatin' (straight) and sittin' (rocking) chairs (pronounced cheers in the hills).

A country auction was a social affair.

The auction

"Feller can't be too careful buyin' at auction."

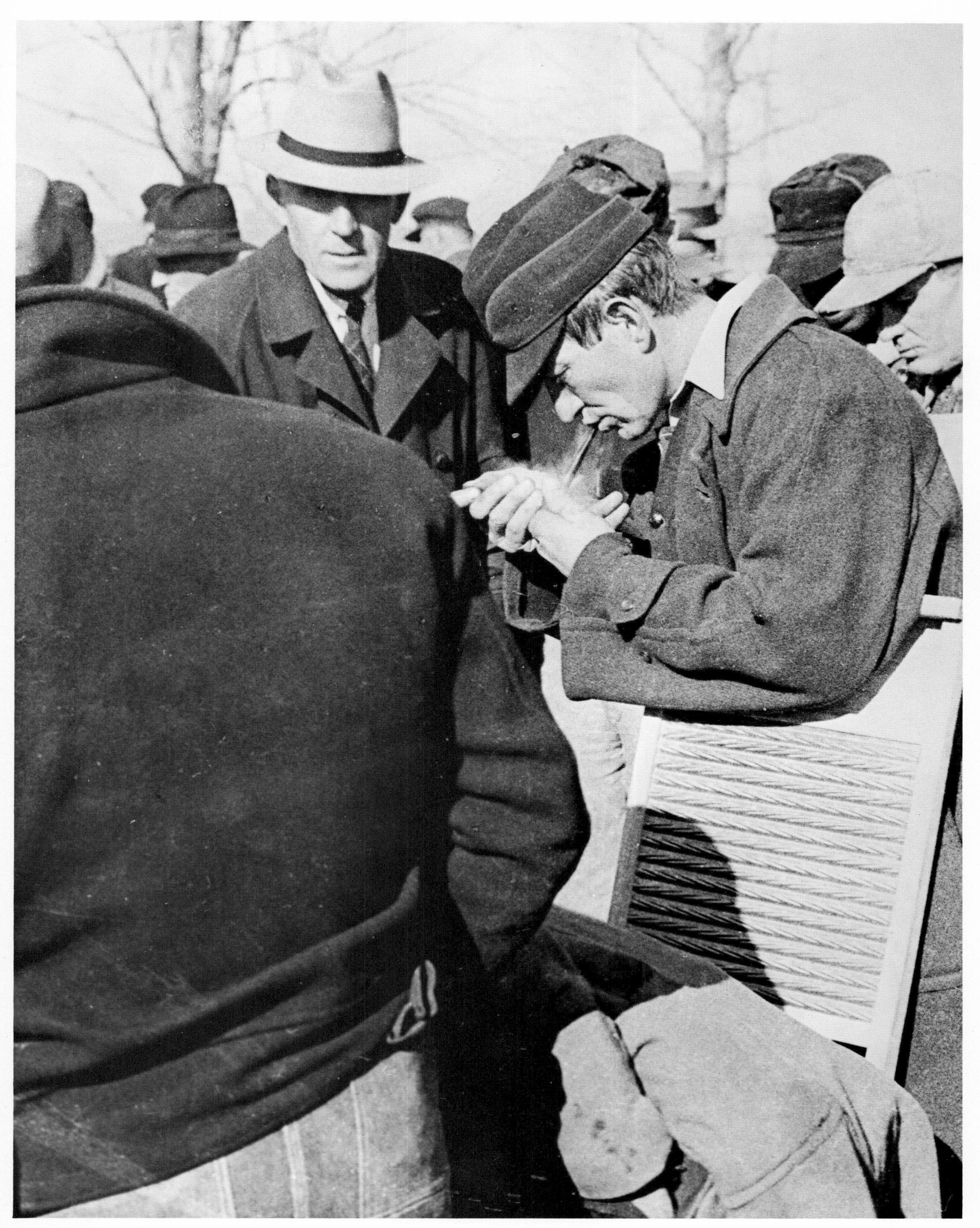

THE BARGAIN HUNTER.

"What am I bid for this fine bull?"

Even the ducks were auctioned off the pond--the buyer had to catch them.

"A body has to pick the bugs off'n a bait of garden sass."

"A feller can take a little loafin' time in the hills."

JUDGE JIM HOLLIDAY knew county elections were won at Fourth of July picnics.

During the recess of a murder trial jurors brought out shape note hymnals from hip pockets and sang spirituals.

Sometimes a man's passions caused him to lose his precious freedom.

AUNT CISSY FINE--weaver.

"Whenever I get to ailin' I drink a sasserful of yarb tea. Hit makes me awful sick. Then I get well and I never been in a hospital in my whole life."

JOHN GROVES: "Life's too hard outside the hills even with the WPA."

Old time religion

In the spirit of his pioneer ancestors John built his own log cabin in which he and his wife raised their children.

Spiritual leader of a pentecostal group on Long Creek, Preacher Groves held brush arbor meetings at the end of each summer.

In the brush arbor.

He preached God's word . . .

directly to his hearers.

"I've helped many a backslider pray through to Jesus and get saved."

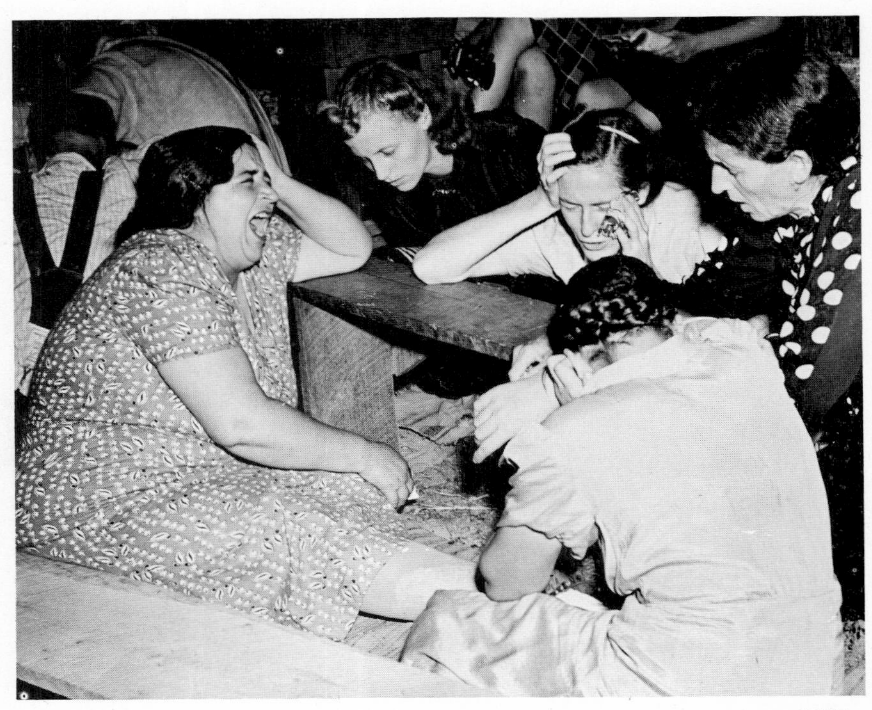

"There's power in the Spirit."

“We’ll gather at the river....”

“Hit’s never too late to pray through.”

"A body's sins are washed clean as a lamb when he goes down in the waters and comes out a new person in Jesus."

"It was a time for rejoicing."

"There's just me an' Old Red left and we're gettin' older ever day. I'm 83 and fightin' to keep out of a nursing home but I don't think my childern 'll ever do that to me.

"Least a feller can do for a neighbor is to make him a coffin."

Burying day

"Folks raised the cotton for the paddin' and stores kept the linin' and the coverin'. We just put the handles on for the looks of things."

An angel crown of feathers formed in the pillow of a dying saintly Ozarker was considered an almost certain passport to heaven. If it were suspected that a crown might be forming, a pillow was not shaken or fluffed lest the crown be disturbed.

"Folks went to the cemetery and took time to hear two preachers and a lot of singin', testifyin', prayin' and weepin'."

In 1843 pioneer Levi Casey from Tennessee built the first of these log houses on Swan Creek just above the creek's mouth on White River. The homestead passed to Amanda Casey who married a McHaffie. One of their children became the wife and mother of bankers.

About the Author-Photographer

TOWNSEND GODSEY, who has had a long career in journalism, left the position of Director of Information and Education for the Missouri Conservation Commission in 1941 and came to the Ozarks to make a photographic record of primitive survivals in the hills. While making this collection of photographs of the last of the old line Ozarkers in their natural environment he supported his family by selling illustrated articles and photo essays to magazines and newspapers and by barter which was one of the ways of sustaining life in the hills during the days of and following the great depression.

He is the author of more than 500 picture stories and articles in publications of national circulation, some 20 plays, three books and three films. Several of his photographs have won national awards.

During the years between the time he collected the photographs in THESE WERE THE LAST, Godsey has earned degrees at Central Missouri State University, the H.H. Herbert School of Journalism at the University of Oklahoma and was awarded an honorary doctoral degree by The School of the Ozarks where for 10 years he was Vice-president for Public Relations and head of the Mass Media department. His teaching career also included years at Stephens College for Women, the Fred Archer School of Photography at Los Angeles and the University of Oklahoma.

Now in his 70's, the author-photographer lives in Branson, Mo., in semi-retirement with his wife, Helen, who collaborates in their production of illustrated articles. She is co-author of the introduction to *These Were the Last*.